Poetry for Students, Volume 39

Project Editor: Sara Constantakis Rights Acquisition and Management: Margaret Chamberlain-Gaston Composition: Evi Abou-El-Seoud Manufacturing: Rhonda Dover Imaging: John Watkins

Product Design: Pamela A. E. Galbreath, Jennifer Wahi Content Conversion: Katrina Coach Product Manager: Meggin Condino

Gale

27500 Drake Rd.

Farmington Hills, MI, 48331-3535

ISBN-13: 978-1-4144-6706-1

ISBN-10: 1-4144-6706-0

ISSN 1094-7019

This title is also available as an e-book.

ISBN-13: 978-1-4144-7390-1

ISBN-10: 1-4144-7390-7

Contact your Gale, a part of Cengage Learning sales representative for ordering information.

Printed in Mexico

1 2 3 4 5 6 7 15 14 13 12 11

Frost at Midnight

Samuel Taylor Coleridge 1798

Introduction

"Frost at Midnight" is a lyrical poem composed by the British author Samuel Taylor Coleridge. Coleridge wrote the poem in 1798, and it was published that same year in his collection *Fears in Solitude*. The year 1798 could be considered something of a high-water mark in English poetry, for that same year Coleridge and his friend and fellow poet William Wordsworth published *Lyrical Ballads. Lyrical Ballads* could arguably be considered one of the most important collections of poetry in the history of English literature. Not only did it launch the careers of Coleridge and Wordsworth, but it also marked a kind of official beginning of the English romantic movement in letters. For the next three decades, some of the most recognizable names in English literature—Wordsworth, Coleridge, Percy Bysshe Shelley, John Keats, George Gordon Lord Byron, Sir Walter Scott—were responsible for an outpouring of poetry (and in the case of Scott, fiction as well) that redefined poetry in English. Much of their work continues to be popular today, not only with literary scholars but with everyday readers as well.

In the twenty-first century, "Frost at Midnight" is unlikely to strike readers as in any way unconventional, daring, or experimental. It is a meditative poem in which the poet uses his observations of nature to reflect on the future of his infant son, who is sleeping nearby as the poet makes those observations. However, in 1798, many readers would have regarded this poem as something almost entirely new in English poetry. Coleridge, along with Wordsworth, was a pioneer in writing a type of poetry that was conversational and informal. The poem is written in blank verse (meaning that it has no rhyme scheme), and the reader senses that the poem records a series of reflections unified by rhythm and imagery rather than by formal poetic devices. The poem can be found in virtually any anthology of romantic poetry, including *The Penguin Book of Romantic Poetry*, edited by Jonathan Wordsworth and Jessica Wordsworth and published by Penguin Books in 2005. The poem can also be found online at the Poetry Foundation Web site.

Author Biography

Coleridge was born on October 21, 1772, at Ottery St. Mary in Devonshire, England. His father was a minister, and in his early years Coleridge inherited his father's scholarly interests. After his father died, Coleridge attended a school called Christ's Hospital in London, where he studied classical writers and was an avid reader. An excellent student, he won a scholarship to Jesus College at Cambridge University, which he attended from 1791 to 1793. His personal life, however, was tumultuous. He was in debt, his health was not good, he associated at Cambridge with political radicals, and he fancied himself desperately in love with the sister of one of his earlier schoolmates. He impulsively left school and joined the army, but his brothers were able to get him discharged and take him back to Cambridge.

In the years that followed, Coleridge became acquainted with other notables in the romantic movement, including Robert Southey and Charles Lamb. He married a woman he did not love, Sara Fricker, who was the sister of Southey's fiance´e. Like most of the figures associated with the romantic movement, he was intrigued by the French Revolution (which had begun in 1789), with its promise of the spread of democracy and the downfall of aristocratic, monarchical forms of government. An idealist, he planned with Southey a utopian community that was to have been set up in

Pennsylvania, but the project came to nothing. He published his first collection of poetry, *Poems on Various Subjects*, in 1796. Sadly, he suffered from bouts of neuralgia (marked by acute, severe, intermittent pain that radiates along nerves). He also suffered from periods of depression. To find relief from the pain and depression, he began to use opium, and he battled an addiction to the drug for the rest of his life.

Coleridge met Wordsworth in 1795. By 1797, the two were intimate friends, and each inspired the other as poets and thinkers, leading to the publication of Coleridge's *Fears in Solitude* (which included "Frost at Midnight") in 1798 and, that same year, of their joint volume, *Lyrical Ballads*. It was during this period that Coleridge wrote many of the poems for which he is most famous, including *The Rime of the Ancient Mariner*, the first part of *Christabel*, and *Kubla Khan*—although a number of the poems he wrote during this period were not published until 1816.

Throughout the years that followed, Coleridge traveled. He spent time in Germany, where he became intrigued with new currents of thought flowing from German philosophers. He spent time on the Mediterranean island of Malta, hoping the warm climate would restore him to health. He also toured Scotland with Wordsworth and his sister, Dorothy. He fell in love with Sarah Hutchinson, the sister of the woman who would later become Wordsworth's wife; he addressed his 1802 poem "Dejection: An Ode" to her. In 1808, he began a series of lectures on literature at England's Royal Institution, and the following year he launched a short-lived literary journal. In 1810, he quarreled with Wordsworth, and although the quarrel was smoothed over, the two men grew apart. These were dark days for Coleridge, for he continued to suffer from poor health, his marriage was a shambles, and he was in debt. He supported himself by journalism, and during the years 1813 to 1816 he lectured on Shakespeare in Bristol, England. He also began work on *Biographia Literaria*, a work of literary criticism. He continued to lecture on literature, and in 1825, he published *Aids to Reflection*, a work of theology. After embarking on another tour of Germany, he published *Constitution of Church and State* in 1830. He died of heart failure in London, England, on July 25, 1834.

Poem Summary

The text used for this summary is from *English Romantic Poetry and Prose*, edited by Russell Noyes, Oxford University Press, 1956, pp. 408–409. Versions of the poem can be found on the following Web pages: http://www.poetryfoundation.org/archive/poem.html id=173242 and http://www.eecs.harvard.edu/~keith/poems/frost.html.

Media Adaptations

- An audio version of "Frost at Midnight" is contained in *English Romantic Poetry*, read by John S. Martin. The recording was made in 1962 by Folkway Records and is available as an MP3 download.

- A more recent audio version of "Frost at Midnight" is part of the collection *Poetry of Samuel Taylor Coleridge*, read by actor Sir Ralph Richardson. The recording was released in 2009 by Saland Publishing and is available as an MP3 download.
- Another audio version of "Frost at Midnight" is contained in the collection *The Richard Burton Poetry Collection*, read by the famed actor Richard Burton. The recording was released in 2010 by Saland Publishing and is available as anMP3 download.

Stanza 1

"Frost at Midnight," consisting of four stanzas of irregular length, is a quiet, meditative poem, ostensibly delivered as the poet sits in his cottage at midnight, his infant son sleeping nearby in his cradle. The first stanza makes clear that it is cold outside, for frost is forming on the window. The poet hears the cry of an owl outside. He emphasizes his solitude, which allows him to meditate. He also emphasizes the calmness of the scene, although he says that the moment is so calm that his thoughts are vexed. He contemplates the natural world outside the cottage, with the ocean, the forests, and the hills, as well as the nearby village, where life goes on unheard, much as dreams are unheard. He calls the reader's attention to the fire in the fireplace, which, at this late hour, is beginning to die out. The only movement in the cottage is the film, or very low flames, fluttering on the fireplace grate; according to English folklore, these films, called strangers, were thought to foreshadow the arrival of an absent friend. The narrator then thinks that the fluttering of the flames in the quiet surroundings creates sympathy between the flames and himself, for he sees his own thoughts as fluttering and inconsistent as well.

Stanza 2

The poet reflects on his days at school, when he had gazed on the bars of a fireplace grate and seen these strangers. He had also had dreams that returned him to his place of birth and its churches. He thinks of the church bells that rang on fair days, calling the ringing of the bells music for poor men. He says that the bells haunted him and made him think of the future. He would continue to gaze at the fire until he slept, and his sleep would lengthen his dreams. The following morning he would continue to gaze at the fire, as though he were studying a book. Sometimes, he says, the door would open partway and his heart would leap, for he believed that a stranger in the form of a townsman, an aunt, or his sister had arrived.

Stanza 3

In the third stanza, the poet directly addresses the sleeping baby. He listens to the baby's gentle breathing, which fills up the vacancy of the calm as well as the gaps in the poet's thoughts. He says that the sight of the baby fills him with happiness and reflects that the baby will grow up to have experiences in other places. The poet notes that he had been brought up in the crowded and dim city, where the only things of beauty he could see were the sky and, at night, the stars. The baby, however, will lead a life in which he can experience nature in the forms of lakes, shores, and mountains, all reflected in the shapes of clouds. The baby will grow up to experience the language of God, who is part of the natural order and teaches people about himself through nature. God, then, will form the child's spirit.

Stanza 4

In the final stanza, the poet expresses the wish that all seasons of the year will be sweet to the child. He hopes that the child can experience the beauty of the green summer and of the winter, when red-breasted birds sing from the snow on the branches of an apple tree and the thatched roofs of cottages steam as the sun melts the snow on them. He continues his reflection on winter by envisioning the fall of water from the eaves and the formation of frost and icicles that shine in the moonlight.

Themes

Nature

One of the chief features of the romantic movement was a heightened interest in the natural world. Beginning in roughly the mid-eighteenth century, poets began to turn their attention to nature. Some poets stressed the solitude and silence of nature, which allowed reflection. Others stressed the grandeur of nature, while still others emphasized nature's changeability. Nature plays a prominent role in "Frost at Midnight." The poet uses the formation of frost on the window as a jumping-off point for his reflections. The poem makes reference to the hooting of an owl, to seas, forests, mountains, and hills, to the quiet of nature, and, in the final stanza, to the passage of the seasons. The poem also contrasts nature, with its simplicity and solitude, with the noise and dirt of the city.

The poet uses these reflections on nature to express the hope that the infant son lying in his cradle nearby will be able to lead a life of simplicity, one that is in tune with nature. In the romantic imagination, the natural world was an expression of the divine, and it was only through contemplation of nature that a person could experience his or her own basic goodness. In contrast, the city, with its crowds, dirt, and artificiality, produced an inauthentic, cramped, unfulfilling life. Contemplation of nature also opened up a person's emotions, intuitive powers, and passions, much as it does in "Frost at Midnight." By tapping into emotions and intuition, according to Coleridge and his contemporaries, a person could avoid living a life limited by reason and rationality and instead lead a life enriched by passion and freedom.

Dreams

The romantic movement, at least in Great Britain, developed as a reaction against the intellectual trends of the seventeenth and eighteenth centuries. This earlier period in English literature is variously referred to as the Age of Reason, the Enlightenment, or sometimes the Augustan Age (referring to the classical writers of ancient Rome under Caesar Augustus). At the risk of oversimplifying, the poetry of this age is best described as being marked by rational thought. It tended to be highly formal, with strict rhyme and metrical schemes (meter is the pattern of stressed and unstressed syllables). The poetry was not contemplative but rather analytical, not enthusiastic but rather cool and measured. Much of the poetry was satiric, as writers used poetry to attack evils or absurdities that they perceived. In these ways, the poetry bore many of the characteristics of the classical poetry of the Augustan Age in ancient Rome (roughly the first century BCE into the first century CE). It was a poetry that appealed more to the mind than to the heart, more to thought than to emotion.

The romantics, in contrast, were more interested in exploring nonrational, emotional states. One way in which they did this was through emphasis on dreams and dreamlike states, for they believed that these states of mind were more human and authentic. Thus, in "Frost at Midnight," the poet enters into a state of contemplation that is almost dreamlike. Clearly, the setting of the poem is the darkness of midnight. He is in a cottage where the only light is provided by the flickering of flames in the fireplace. The surroundings induce in him a trancelike state that allows his mind to wander. He sees in the flames of the fireplace a "stranger" that touches on his romantic longings. In the second stanza, Coleridge refers explicitly to dreams when he reflects on his earlier life at school and how he would dream. He talks about the gaps between thought. Thought is rational, but it is in the gaps between thinking that genuine, authentic experience is to be had. Very often for the romantics, these gaps were dreams, trances, and moments of undisciplined contemplation, where truth and insight could be achieved.

Father-Child Relationships

"Frost at Midnight" is in some sense an autobiographical poem. The voice of the poem is that of Coleridge himself, and although he does not name his infant son in the poem, that infant was in fact his son, Hartley. Throughout the poem,

Coleridge expresses his wish that his son will lead a life that will allow him to contemplate the wonders of the natural world. His reflections on his son induce him to think about his own childhood, particularly his time at school.

Topics for Further Study

- Research the history of the French Revolution, which began with the storming of the Bastille prison in Paris in 1789. Think about why there were so many writers, artists, and philosophers in England (and elsewhere) buoyed by the revolution. Why did it tend to fuel their sense of optimism? Present your findings in a report or presentation.
- The names of both Coleridge and his friend Wordsworth are often

associated with the Lake District, a region in northwest England. In fact, the two are sometimes referred to as the "Lake poets." Conduct Internet and traditional research on the Lake District. Find images of the Lake District, particularly those of spots in the region that the poets frequented (for example, Grasmere and Rydal Mount), and share them with your classmates in a digital format using PowerPoint or SlideShare. Explain to your classmates how the Lake District might have inspired the romantic poets.

- What was the romantic movement in English literature? Conduct research on the history of the romantic movement. Prepare an interactive digital timeline or a traditional poster board timeline that includes the movement's major authors and works. Supplement your time line with works written by non-English authors. (Germany was a source of inspiration for the romantic writers.)

- A prominent poet in the American Harlem Renaissance (a flowering of literature, art, and music in New York City's Harlem neighborhood in the 1910s and 1920s and beyond) was Countee Cullen, who often looked to the romantics for his inspiration. Locate a copy of Cullen's poem "Saturday's Child" (available online at http://www.poetryfoundation.org/archive id=171340), a lyric poem suitable for young-adult readers that touches on the relationship between a father and his child, born into the poverty of an African American community. Write an essay that contrasts the vision and aspirations for the next generation contained in this poem and "Frost at Midnight." Post your essay to the class blog and invite your classmates to comment on your opinions.

- Conduct Internet and traditional research on Coleridge's proposed utopian community, which he planned to create with fellow writer Robert Southey. What was the name of the proposed community? Where was it to be located? On what principles was it to be run? Why did the project never come to fruition? Most importantly, what was the appeal of such a community to a romantic poet like Coleridge? Share your findings with your classmates in a multimedia presentation.

After his father's death in 1781, Coleridge, still just a boy, was sent to a London school called Christ's Hospital, a charity school founded in the sixteenth century. He was rarely allowed to return home, and he spent his time reading—everything from classical writers such as Virgil (a Roman writer) to the tales of the Arabian Nights. In London, he would rarely have had opportunity to experience the beauties of nature, particularly since London at that time tended to be crowded, noisy, smelly, crime-ridden, and dirty, with ramshackle housing (with few windows, because windows were taxed), lack of clean water, and an appalling lack of sanitation. (For example, dead animals were often left to rot in the streets, and most people disposed of their human waste by simply emptying chamber pots out onto the streets.)

Coleridge touches on his sense of loneliness and isolation at school in London and his wish for something better. He transfers this wish to his infant son, hoping that his son will be able to experience the beauties of nature, with its hills, forests, streams, lakes, mountains, and the like. In this way, his son will be able to understand the language of God and allow God to mold his spirit. Coleridge's views are characteristic of the views of the romantics, who tended to see themselves as living at the dawn of a new age of freedom, artistic endeavor, and the fulfillment of utopian dreams.

Style

Blank verse

The term *blank verse* is used loosely to refer to any poetry that does not rhyme. Strictly speaking, though, blank verse refers to unrhymed poetry using the metrical form called iambic pentameter. Iambic pentameter lines are composed of metrical units consisting of five two syllable feet with the first syllable unaccented, the second accented. This is the metrical form used in "Frost at Midnight."

An examination of the lines shows that most of them consist of ten syllables, or five metrical feet, although there are exceptions, with some lines containing eleven syllables. Further, the general pattern is for an unaccented syllable to be followed by an accented syllable, although again, there are variations. Blank verse was a metrical form favored by the romantics (and in fact widely used since the sixteenth century by poets, including Shakespeare) because it mirrors the rhythms of natural English speech, particularly because it was flexible. It accommodated, for example, an extra syllable or variations in the pattern of accented and unaccented syllables. It also gave the poet freedom to allow the grammar of a sentence to spill over from one line into the next: lines did not have to end with periods or commas that mark a break in the sentence structure.

In this way, romantic poetry in general differed from the poetry of the Enlightenment, which tended to adhere strictly to a metrical form, one in which units of lines corresponded strictly with the grammatical units of a sentence. "Frost at Midnight" is often referred to as a conversational poem, and the romantics often wrote poetry that was conversational in tone. Although Coleridge was hardly original in his use of blank verse, he used its flexibly to create poems that were organized not by form but by the play of his mind as he contemplated experience.

Imagery

An image is a concrete representation of an object or sensory experience. Typically, imagery refers to visual sensory experience, but imagery can also be used to represent sounds and smells. Sometimes, imagery is literal; that is, the images have no particular meaning beyond their obvious denotation. Sometimes, imagery is figurative, meaning that it extends the obvious meaning of the words. The romantic poets, including Coleridge, placed great emphasis on precise observation in their delineations of the natural world, and therefore their poetry is filled with visual and other forms of imagery. In "Frost at Midnight," Coleridge relies primarily on literal imagery. He wants to recreate for the reader the physical details surrounding him and that he recalls from his earlier days. Much of this imagery is visual: he takes note of the frost, the moon, icicles, and other natural phenomena, as well as the fluttering of the flames in the fireplace and the steam rising from snow melting on a thatched rooftop. Some of the imagery is aural, including the hoot of an owl and the tolling of church bells that he remembers from his school days. All of this imagery comes together to create a portrait of a poet who allows himself to observe in detail his surroundings and use those surroundings as fuel for contemplation.

Interior monologue

Interior monologue is a narrative technique in which a character's thoughts are revealed in a way that appears to be uncontrolled by the author. The interior monologue typically aims to reveal the inner self of a character. It portrays emotional experiences as they occur at both conscious and unconscious levels. Images are often used to represent sensations or emotions. Typically, the term is used in discussions of fiction, where authors use the technique to reveal the state of mind of a character. The term, however, can also be applied to a poem that is written to accomplish the same end. The reader is invited to imagine the speaker of the poem as a character, set in a certain situation, who reveals his thoughts and emotions through the lines of the poem.

In this sense, "Frost at Midnight" bears many of the characteristics of an interior monologue. The "character" is seated in his cottage. The time is midnight or thereabouts. It is cold outside, so a fire burns in the fireplace. Near the speaker is his infant son, asleep. The scene, with its quiet and isolation, prompts musing on the part of the poet. He observes the frost forming on the window and the flickering of the fire in the fireplace. He meditates about the natural surroundings and the nearby village. These musings prompt him then to think about his own childhood and the role of dreams in his life when he was at school. This in turn prompts him to think about his upbringing and to draw a contrast between life in the crowded city and life surrounded by the beauties of the natural world. These reflections then forge in him the hope that his son will be able to grow up surrounded by these beauties and that God, as reflected in nature and conceived of as a teacher, will mold the son's spirit.

Historical Context

Age of Revolution

"Frost at Midnight" makes no reference to historical events. However, historical events in the late 1700s played a major role in influencing the thinking of the romantic poets in England and throughout Europe. British writers such as Coleridge would have followed events on the European continent closely, and those events had a profound impact on the romantics.

During the late eighteenth century, powerful intellectual trends were at work in Europe. These trends would sweep away tradition and give rise to revolutionary sentiments. The first of these revolutions took place against Great Britain in what would become the birth of the United States in 1775. The second was the revolution in France which erupted when Parisians stormed the Bastille prison in 1789. What followed was years of turmoil in France as the nation attempted to install a revolutionary government that ended the monarchy, curbed aristocratic privilege, broke the monopoly of the Catholic Church, and provided citizens with a greater measure of political equality.

Compare & Contrast

- **1790s**: Education often takes place

in the homes of the upper classes or the homes of members of such professions as the law or the ministry. Many students are sent away from home to boarding schools for varying lengths of time. Typically, only boys receive formal schooling.

Today: Although boarding schools continue to operate, most students attend public or private schools in their community while living at home, and formal schooling is available equally to boys and girls.

- **1790s**: Opium, much of it imported from China, is legal and often self-administered by people with illnesses, pain, or depression; many women take opium to relieve menstrual discomfort, and opium in the form of laudanum is often given to teething infants and irritable children. A significant number of people are addicted to opium, which they usually ingest in the form of a tincture (liquid medicine), but this type of drug addiction, while discouraged, is not highly stigmatized.

  Today: Medicines made with opiates (morphine, for example) are highly regulated and legally available only through prescription from a doctor—and then only to alleviate the most serious pain. The most common illegally used opiate is heroin, and addiction to this type of drug is highly stigmatized.

- **1790s**: The population of London is just under one million. The city has no sanitary facilities, and waste is dumped into the river Thames, which is the source of the city's drinking water. Many people die or become seriously ill with infectious diseases caused by impure water and lack of sanitation.
  Today: The population of London is about 7.8 million people. Like any modern city in a developed nation, London provides clean water and sewage treatment, sharply diminishing the incidence of infectious disease.

Artists and philosophers called for a return to nature and promoted the belief in the inherent goodness of people, providing intellectual support for revolutionary fervor. In France, one of the most influential writers was Jean-Jacques Rousseau, who began the body of his 1762 essay *Du contrat social* (On the Social Contract) with the words: “Man is born free, and everywhere he is in chains.” He began his 1762 novel *E´mile* with the words: “God makes all things good; man meddles with them and they become evil." The subtitle of *Émile* is *ou, De l' éducation* (Or, On Education), and the novel goes on to depict a child of nature who lives a simple country life, his senses attuned to the natural world. While these and other books by Rousseau and other writers did not call for revolution, they planted in people's minds the seeds of revolt against a repressive, artificial, established order. In a very real sense, Coleridge's musings in "Frost at Midnight" and his longing that his son, too, be a child of nature can be traced back to the viewpoints Rousseau made popular in France and that provided, in part, the intellectual underpinnings for the French Revolution.

In England, attitudes toward the French Revolution were mixed. Writers such as Coleridge and Wordsworth were excited by the lofty goals of the revolution. They believed that the revolution represented the liberation of mankind. However, like many people in England, they were revolted by the violent turn the revolution took. Political radicals in France attempted to impose a stifling uniformity on French revolutionary society, and during the Reign of Terror, numerous aristocrats—and people who supported the aristocracy (or were thought to)—were executed.

In the wake of the revolution, Napoleon Bonaparte seized control of the nation. From the 1790s until his death in 1821, he led armies in an effort to sweep away monarchies in Europe and spread the ideals of the revolution. Although revolution dominated events on the continent during these years, England escaped revolution—although many Britons feared a Napoleonic invasion. Despite the political turmoil, warfare, and violence that attended the French Revolution, the revolution fired the idealism of English romantics. In his poem "France: An Ode," written in 1798, Coleridge expressed a common view when he stated that France fervently desired to be free and that he felt both hope and fear as a result of the French Revolution.

Critical Overview

While "Frost at Midnight" is not one of Coleridge's major poems, it generally has been held in high regard by critics and scholars. Among his contemporaries, the opinion expressed by a reviewer for the *British Critic* in 1799 is typical. The reviewer writes that the poem "is entitled to much praise. A few affectations of phraseology, are atoned for by much expressive tenderness, and will be avoided by the author's more mature judgment."

More recent critics and scholars have expressed similar admiration for the poem. Arden Reed, in his essay "Frost at Midnight," writes:

> Recent criticism has generally presented the poem as one of Coleridge's rare imaginative successes, pointing out the speaker's increasing awareness and the poem's growth in "organic unity" as it rounds back upon itself to form a perfect circle.

Similarly, Stephen Prickett, in *Coleridge and Wordsworth: The Poetry of Growth*, calls "Frost at Midnight" "one of his finest poems." Prickett continues by pointing out that

> the associative drift of his mind reveals itself in a series of contrasts. The cold calm of the present night is

details of their attack on the traditional Church.

He frowned a little, thrust out his chin, and then smiled again.

"I was w...wondering when some of these would turn up. I thought it might happen later—in Rome. You see it's important you understand that the Church is never free of corruption, and that the devil is not just an abstraction. The spiritual world is one of serious conflict."

"But what about them? Shouldn't someone be trying to save them?"

"A beautiful Catholic thought, Bridge. But it's probably not for you to take this on while you're at this point on your journey. Our Lord said to his disciples that some evil can only be cured by prayer and fasting. It is the sort of case we should entrust to serious contemplatives like the Carthusians. But when we have the opportunity we should include them in our prayers. Of course God never despairs of anyone.

"But let us take the Metro and meet those young people who represent the future of the Church in France, and not allow ourselves to be depressed by a corrupt element of it emanating out of Montreal. The reassuring thing to remember is that those who peddle false doctrine and ideas in the Church have never been able to persuade the young to follow them for long. In every sense they are sterile."

Our Metro journey to the Parc Monceau involved several changes and took rather longer than I had expected. Benson used the time to explain that our *rendez-vous* was at this park because it was near where the family of one of the students had their apartment.

I was still disturbed by my encounter with the French Canadian priests. I used our journey to ask Benson what should be my attitude if I found myself at a Mass celebrated by one of these priests. I said that I fervently hoped that this might never happen, but, perhaps if I did come to see more of the Catholic Church, I could foresee being faced with a similar kind of priest, or a bizarre form of liturgy full of modern accretions and excesses.

> juxtaposed with the bells of Ottery St Mary on a hot summer fair-day in his childhood. His own childhood is seen, in turn, through the bored nostalgia of the schoolboy at Christ's Hospital.

In his essay “Coleridge and Wordsworth: Collaboration and Criticism from *Salisbury Plain* to *Aids to Reflection*,” Richard Gravil calls “Frost at Midnight” one of “the very greatest poems of 1798” and praises the poem for its “perfected ruminative tone.” Michael O' Neill, in his essay “Coleridge's Genres,” writes that the poem “delights by offering itself as a process, a reverie, that with miraculous delicacy ends up as an artistically organized product.”

Paul Magnuson, in his essay “The ‘Conversation’ Poems,” writes: “In the ‘Conversation’ poems, Coleridge adopts a natural symbolism in which the perceiving, remembering, imagining mind searches for images of itself and God in nature.” Also, in contrast to some earlier nature poets, Coleridge can “deepen the psychological insight and the philosophical meditations on the relation of the mind to nature.”

Finally, in *Samuel Taylor Coleridge*, Virginia L. Radley discusses “Frost at Midnight” in conjunction with “This Lime-Tree Bower My Prison.” She writes:

> Although no conversation poem can rightly be said to stand equally with

the poems of high imagination [including *Kubla Khan* and *The Rime of the Ancient Mariner*], … certainly "Frost at Midnight" and "This Lime-Tree Bower …" both have within them that quality of heart so essential to these latter poems. Because of this quality, and because of the striking effectiveness of their imagery, these poems can be said to be the true harbingers of Coleridge's greatest poems.

What Do I Read Next?

- Coleridge's "This Lime-Tree Bower My Prison," written in 1797, bears many similarities to "Frost at Midnight." Because of an injury, the speaker is unable to join his companions in a walking tour, but while sitting in a bower of lime trees is able to reflect vicariously on the beauty and divinity of nature through their experience. The poem can be found in *The Penguin Book of Romantic Poetry*, edited by Jonathan Wordsworth and Jessica Wordsworth and published by Penguin Books in 2005.

- William Wordsworth's "The World Is Too Much with Us," written in about 1802, is a sonnet that expresses themes common to the romantic poets, including the belief that modern city life is corrupting and that a life surrounded by nature is superior. The poem can be found in *The Penguin Book of Romantic Poetry*, edited by Jonathan Wordsworth and Jessica Wordsworth and published by Penguin Books in 2005.
- Students interested in fictional treatments of the French Revolution would enjoy Kimberly Brubaker Bradley's *The Lacemaker and the Princess* (2007), a young-adult novel that narrates the events of the French Revolution both from the aristocratic side (the princess) and from the viewpoint of a common person (the lacemaker).

- Students interested in historical treatments of the French Revolution might begin with Laura K. Egendorg's *The French Revolution* (2003), a volume in the Greenhaven Press's "Opposing Viewpoints in World History" series suitable for young adults. The book presents both primary and secondary sources that offer different perspectives on the event that permanently altered Europe.
- Another major English romantic poet was Percy Bysshe Shelley, whose poem "Mont Blanc," written in 1816, is a reflection on the power and majesty of nature as represented by Mont Blanc, located between France and Italy and the highest mountain peak in the Alps. The poem can be found in *The Penguin Book of Romantic Poetry*, edited by Jonathan Wordsworth and Jessica Wordsworth and published by Penguin Books in 2005.
- After the romantic movement spread to Spain, Gustavo Adolfo Be´cquer emerged as one of the leading Spanish romantic poets. He was the author of two collections, *Rimas* (Poems) and *Leyendas* (Legends). The works are available in Spanish

in a 2007 collection, *Rimas y Leyendas*, published by Edimat Libros, and selections from the works can be found in a 2006 dual Spanish-English edition by the same title; the pieces are translated into English by Stanley Appelbaum, and the book is published by Dover Publications. Each of the poems and legends is quite brief.

- Readers interested in contemporary poetry for young adults about nature could begin with *Poems for a Small Planet: Contemporary American Nature Poetry* (1993), edited by Robert Pack and Jay Parini. Readers can compare and contrast attitudes toward nature in modern life with those of the eighteenth-and nineteenth-century romantic writers such as Coleridge.

Sources

Coleridge, Samuel Taylor, "France: An Ode," in *English Romantic Poetry and Prose*, edited by Russell Noyes, Oxford University Press, 1956, p. 410.

Coleridge, Samuel Taylor, "Frost at Midnight," in *English Romantic Poetry and Prose*, edited by Russell Noyes, Oxford University Press, 1956, pp. 408–409.

Gravil, Richard, "Coleridge and Wordsworth: Collaboration and Criticism from *Salisbury Plain* to *Aids to Reflection*," in *The Oxford Handbook of Samuel Taylor Coleridge*, edited by Frederick Burwick, Oxford University Press, 2009, pp. 24, 26.

"London, 1800–1913," in *The Proceedings of the Old Bailey*, http://www.oldbaileyonline.org/static/Londonlife19t (accessed April 6, 2011).

Magnuson, Paul, "The 'Conversation' Poems," in *The Cambridge Companion to Coleridge*, edited by Lucy Newlyn, Cambridge University Press, 2002, p. 34.

Noyes, Russell, ed., *English Romantic Poetry and Prose*, Oxford University Press, 1956, pp. xix—xxxiii, 373–79, 408–410.

O' Neill, Michael, "Coleridge's Genres," in *The Oxford Handbook of Samuel Taylor Coleridge*, edited by Frederick Burwick, Oxford University

Press, 2009, p. 381.

Prickett, Stephen, *Coleridge and Wordsworth: The Poetry of Growth*, Cambridge University Press, 1970, pp. 47, 49.

Radley, Virginia L., *Samuel Taylor Coleridge*, Twayne Publishers, 1966, p. 56.

Reed, Arden, "Frost at Midnight," in *Samuel Taylor Coleridge*, edited by Harold Bloom, Chelsea House Publishers, 1986, pp. 191–92.

Review of "Frost at Midnight" in *Samuel Taylor Coleridge: The Critical Heritage*, edited by J. R. de J. Jackson, Barnes & Noble, 1970, p. 49; originally published in *British Critic*, June 1799, pp. 662–63.

Rousseau, Jean-Jacques, *E mile*, in *Literature Network*, http://www.online-literature.com/rousseau/emile/1/ (accessed April 6, 2011).

Rousseau, Jean-Jacques, *The Social Contract*, in *Literature Network*, http://www.online-literature.com/rousseau/social-contractor-principles-/2/ (accessed April 6, 2011).

"2009 Round Demographic Projections for the London Plan (Revised)," in *Greater London Authority Intelligence Update*, http://www.london.gov.uk/sites/default/files/dmag/U 2010%202009%20Round%20Demographic%20Proj (accessed April 6, 2011).

Further Reading

Arnold, James R., *The Aftermath of the French Revolution*, Twenty-First Century Books, 2008.

As the title suggests, this volume focuses on the effects of the French Revolution. It traces how the revolution created the expectation that countries could be ruled by democratic governments, without hereditary kings and queens who exercised arbitrary power. The book demonstrates how the revolution gave rise to the middle class, diminished the power of the church, ended feudalism, and created a new, more modern sense of national identity.

Ashton, Rosemary, *The Life of Samuel Taylor Coleridge: A Critical Biography*, Wiley-Blackwell, 1998.

This volume not only provides details about the author's life, but as a critical biography, it links that life to his works. Readers interested in such facets of the author's life as his opium addiction, his literary criticism, and his marital relationship will find a wealth of information here.

Cranston, Maurice, *The Romantic Movement*, Wiley-Blackwell, 1994.

This relatively brief book discusses the romantic movement not just as a British phenomenon but as a European one. The author focuses on how romanticism manifested itself in England, Italy, Spain, and Germany and locates the characteristics that romanticism in these countries had in common despite their national differences: an emphasis on liberty, introspection, and the exotic.

Plantinga, Leon, *Romantic Music: A History of Musical Style in Nineteenth-Century Europe*, Norton, 1984.

The romantic movement extended to other artistic forms, including painting and music. Readers interested in the romantic era of music, which included such composers as Beethoven, Schubert, Liszt, and others, will find in this volume discussion of how romanticism and the intellectual trends that supported it found expression in music.

Suggested Search Terms

Coleridge AND religion

eighteenth-century London

English romantic movement

French Revolution

Frost at Midnight

Jean-Jacques Rousseau

Lyrical Ballads AND Coleridge AND Wordsworth

romantic movement

romanticism AND nature

Samuel Taylor Coleridge

William Wordsworth

Frost at Midnight AND Coleridge

romanticism AND Coleridge

Coleridge AND Wordsworth

Lightning Source UK Ltd.
Milton Keynes UK
UKHW021458250719
346804UK00006B/881/P

9 781375 380355